The Audition

by Barbara A. Donovan
illustrated by Amanda Haley

Harcourt
SCHOOL PUBLISHERS

Printed in the United States of America

ISBN 10: 0-15-351688-7
ISBN 13: 978-0-15-351688-7

Ordering Options
ISBN 10: 0-15-351216-4 (Grade 6 Advanced Collection)
ISBN 13: 978-0-15-351216-2 (Grade 6 Advanced Collection)
ISBN 10: 0-15-358171-9 (package of 5)
ISBN 13: 978-0-15-358171-7 (package of 5)

1 2 3 4 5 6 7 8 9 10 179 12 11 10 09 08 07 06

The announcement was pinned to the bulletin board in Madame Belle's Dance Studio. It held the words Niabi had hoped for, dreamed of, and worked towards since she had started ballet classes when she was only four years old. There would be an audition of dancers for one of the most popular ballets of all time—*The Nutcracker*. Niabi could barely breathe as she read the announcement and recalled the tryouts last year.

"You should try out for the part of Clara," whispered a voice behind Niabi.

Niabi knew the voice belonged to another dance student, Alyssa. "What good would that do, Alyssa?" Niabi asked. "You know that you are the best ballet student in this studio. You're probably the best in the whole city. Why should I try out for a starring part when I haven't got a chance of winning it?"

Alyssa was silent for a minute. Then she said, "You never know what will happen during a tryout, Niabi. You could give a perfect performance. Something could go haywire with mine. Then you would win the role."

Blood rushed to Niabi's face as she remembered her horrible tryout last year for *The Nutcracker*. She turned to face Alyssa, but she had already walked away. Niabi's shoulders slumped as she recalled the most embarrassing moment of her life.

Last year at the audition, the director was telling each girl to take certain ballet positions. Each dancer before Niabi had been dismissed, and Niabi had thought all of them to be better dancers than she was. She couldn't believe she had made it this far. Then, when it was her turn, she froze. It was like her feet were fused to the floor. She was immobile for about thirty seconds before the director cut in. With a weary intonation, he said, "Next!" Niabi, too, had been dismissed.

Adjusting her dance bag on her shoulder and straightening her back, Niabi strode into the studio. Madame Belle was teaching the *en pointe* class today. It would not do for her teacher to see Niabi looking less than confident. As Madame Belle often pointed out, she had no time for students who were not serious about dance. According to Madame Belle, if you were serious about dance, you always carried yourself with the self-confidence of a star.

Niabi began her warm-up exercises at the *barre*, the horizontal bar used by dancers for exercise. Luckily, Alyssa was not next to her, so there would be no further talk about the auditions. As Niabi fluidly moved her supple limbs through the positions that Madame Belle called out, her brain returned to thoughts of the tryouts. This year she would be more prepared than last year. Also, she was in her second year of dancing *en pointe*. To dance the part of Clara, you had to be very good at dancing on your toes. Niabi was taking three *en pointe* classes each week plus all her other ballet classes. Maybe she was ready to give it another try. What was the point of taking ten hours of dance classes each week if she was never going to be able to try out for a part with a real ballet company?

As Madame Belle finished the *barre* exercises, the class moved into the center of the floor for more work. Here the dancers did not have the *barre* for support. Here they had to stand on their toes and leap and turn as though they were the lightest feathers tossed into the air by a gentle breeze. Whenever Niabi lifted off her toes, she imagined herself as a fawn delicately leaping over a log. In Niabi's Native American language, her name meant "fawn."

The ten girls in the class formed two lines of five girls each. Alyssa ended up in the spot directly behind Niabi. Alyssa whispered, "Niabi, it wasn't a jest about the audition. I really think you should try out for the part of Clara. I really do!"

Madame Belle sharply rapped her cane on the floor. She demanded that Alyssa share with the entire class the message that was so important that she had to interrupt the class to share it. Alyssa blushed. She told her teacher that she had just been suggesting to Niabi that she try out for the part of Clara in *The Nutcracker*. Madame Belle stared at both girls for a full ten seconds before saying, "I agree." Then she returned to the dance routines without another word about it.

For the remainder of the class, Niabi's mind whirled around the idea that Madame Belle thought she was ready for the part of Clara. It was a far-fetched idea. In fact, it was quite possibly the silliest idea of the century, but if Madame Belle agreed . . .

After class, Niabi sat on a bench unwinding the ribbons from her *pointe* shoes. Alyssa hovered near her. "Hey, Niabi, I am very sorry," Alyssa began. "I did not mean for Madame Belle to hear me. I didn't mean to embarrass you, but I really think you ought to try out for the part."

Niabi looked up from her shoes and said, "Why should I try out for a part that you're sure to get?"

Alyssa stared at the ceiling. She took a deep breath before saying, "I am not supposed to say anything yet, but my parents might take me out of school for a week at the end of November. There's going to be a huge family reunion thousands of miles from here. If we go, I'll miss several rehearsals. I'll also miss the dress rehearsal. You know what that means."

Niabi nodded her head. She did, indeed, know what that meant. The directors of the ballet made it very clear. If you could not make every rehearsal and every performance for which you were scheduled to dance, don't bother trying out.

"That's awful," said Niabi truthfully. "Don't your parents know that you are sure to get the part of Clara?"

"Yes, they know," admitted Alyssa. "They have made tons of sacrifices for me to study dance all these years. It is important to them that I go to the reunion, and I don't want them to miss it either. Besides, I've danced in *The Nutcracker* for the past several years. I was a mouse twice, a snowflake, and a soldier."

"This year is your big chance, though."

"It's fine," said Alyssa. "Just think—I'll be an *even* better Clara next year. Anyway, my parents haven't decided yet. I just may be able to try out after all. That shouldn't affect you. You should try out. You have made great progress this year."

"I'll think about it," Niabi promised. "Thanks."

That night as Niabi lay in bed, she gazed at her favorite poster. It showed Maria Tallchief, the famous Native American ballet dancer. Maria Tallchief had danced in *The Nutcracker*, as well as many other ballets. What would she have done if she had had a terrible audition like Niabi's? Niabi thought she knew the answer. Still, she argued with herself about it.

The next morning, Niabi counted out five dollars from her piggy bank. She went on-line, printed an application for *The Nutcracker*, and brought it to the breakfast table. If her parents would sign it and write a check for the five-dollar fee, then she'd like to try out for *The Nutcracker* again. Niabi's parents were excited that she was willing to take a chance again. They would have supported her no matter what she did, but they were proud that she was willing to fight for what she wanted.

On Saturday at her *en pointe* class, Niabi spotted Alyssa. Alyssa didn't see her because she was busy tying the ribbons on her shoes. Niabi stood in front of her and held out her hand. "Thanks," Niabi said. Alyssa looked puzzled but shook Niabi's hand anyway. "I've decided to try out for the part of Clara."

A slow smile crept across Alyssa's face. "Then the part will be yours," she said. "My parents have decided to go to the reunion after all."

Niabi sat down beside Alyssa. She began putting on her own shoes. "I'm sorry to hear that. I decided that I needed to try even if I had to compete against you. If I want to be a dancer, then I must go to auditions. I need to be tougher. I have to get over my fears."

Alyssa nodded. "You'll do fine. I have been to plenty of auditions. If you need help, just let me know."

"Thanks. I will," said Niabi.

All through her dance class, Niabi thought about what Alyssa had said. Once the class was over, she rushed to Alyssa's side. She asked, "Would you really help me get ready for *The Nutcracker* auditions?"

A warm smile lit up Alyssa's face. "You bet I will! If I can't have the part, then you should have it. I think Madame Belle will even let us use an empty practice room. Let's check with her. Then we can make a plan."

Niabi's eyes gleamed with happiness. Madame Belle had agreed to let them use a small room right away. They went to the room and stood in first position in front of the mirrors. Their fingers lightly touched the *barre* for support. Easily, they stretched onto their toes. "I'll call out the positions," Alyssa said. "You follow."

One by one, Alyssa named the positions. She stood behind Niabi and watched her gracefully flex her legs. She checked the curve of her arms and hands. She watched the way she held her body each time. "Perfect!" Alyssa said after twenty minutes. "Now let's switch places. Pretend you are at the audition, and I am the person in front of you. The director is calling out the positions. Begin!"

This time as Alyssa called out the positions, she exaggerated the way she made them. Sometimes she added her own movements to the positions. In the mirror, she watched Niabi copy her. "No, no, no!" Alyssa finally said. "You watched me, instead of listening to the director."

Niabi looked confused. "I followed just what you did!" she cried. "How could that be wrong?"

Alyssa sighed. "Most directors don't want you to be creative for these kinds of auditions. They want to know that you can make and hold each position. Later, after you get the part, they might tell you the creative changes they want you to make.

Here's my biggest tip for you: *Never watch what the other dancers do*. The director will call out the positions for other girls to perform. You close your eyes. You picture in your mind how *you* would do them. Don't let the flourishes—or mistakes—of the other dancers get into your head. Let's try it again. This time, do what the director says. Do not copy me."

After another twenty minutes, Alyssa said, "That was better. Next time we'll do *centre* work, too."

The following week, Niabi and Alyssa worked together almost every day. During their *centre* work, Alyssa led Niabi through a series of sinuous steps and turns. Sometimes the steps were slow to show off Niabi's sense of balance. They displayed her control of her body, too. Other routines had her spinning, leaping, and turning like a top.

On the day before the audition, Alyssa believed that Niabi was as ready as she could be. Niabi was less certain. She begged Alyssa to come with her to the audition, but Alyssa couldn't go. She had a dance class that she could not miss since she would be missing so many classes while she was away.

"What if I freeze again like last year?" cried Niabi. "Sure I know all the steps and positions, but I'm afraid—"

"Don't be afraid. That's the point. You are as prepared to try out for this part as you can be. If you feel like you are slipping back into your old ways, then stop. Take a cleansing breath. Breathe in deeply. Hold it for a few seconds. Who is your favorite dancer?"

"Maria Tallchief," Niabi said without hesitation.

"Then while you are holding that cleansing breath, picture yourself as Maria Tallchief. Holding in your breath lifts up your head. Let your breath out slowly. Make your posture that of your favorite dancer. Be Maria Tallchief. Let all the other sights and sounds of the hall fade away. Make it so that only you and the director are on the stage."

"How do you know that will work?" Niabi asked.

"I know it works because it's what I do for every audition. You are not the only one who gets nervous, you know," Alyssa confessed with a smile.

Niabi took a deep breath. She pictured herself as Maria Tallchief dancing in *The Nutcracker*. As she let her breath out, she felt taller and stronger. She felt more confident. She could do this after all.

Think Critically

1. How are Alyssa and Niabi alike and different?

2. Why do you think Niabi admires Maria Tallchief?

3. What does Niabi mean when she says that her parents have made "tons of sacrifices" for her to study dance?

4. Why do you think Madame Belle hesitated before giving her answer about whether Niabi should try out for the part of Clara?

5. What do you think happened at Niabi's audition this time?

Performing Arts

Ballet and More There are many different types of dance in addition to ballet. Research various types of dance, such as tap, jazz, ballroom, swing, and modern. Make a chart that lists what is important in each type of dance. Then decide which type of dance you would most like to learn.

School-Home Connection Summarize this story for a family member. Then turn on some music and dance together.

Word Count: 2,168